Contents

Body parts

wax crayon

big sheet of paper

❈ Ask a friend to lie down on the paper.

❈ Draw around their body with a wax crayon.

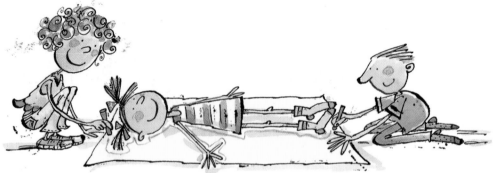

❈ Label these body parts on your picture.

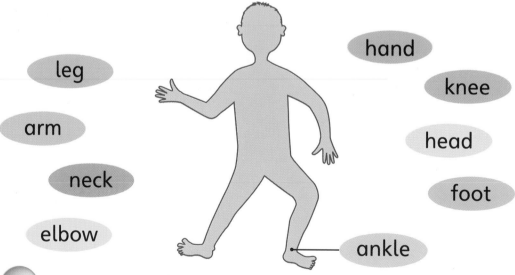

leg

hand

knee

arm

head

neck

foot

elbow

ankle

Head parts

These children are
writing the names
of parts of the body.

Write the names of parts of the head on
Task Sheet 1.

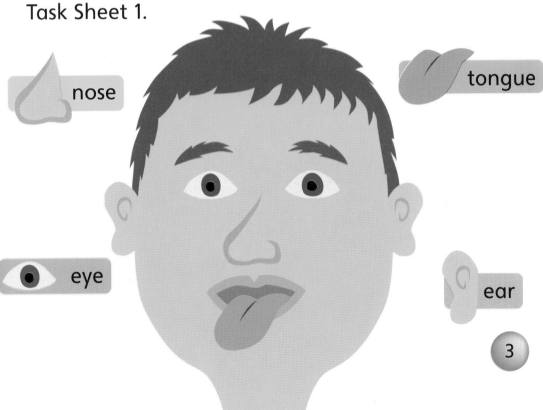

nose

tongue

eye

ear

3

Using senses

These children are playing a game.

They are using different senses to help them guess the objects.

✿ Which senses are they using?

✿ Try some tests like these.

✿ Which sense did you use?

✿ Draw and write the sense you used for each test.

✿ Use pictures like these.

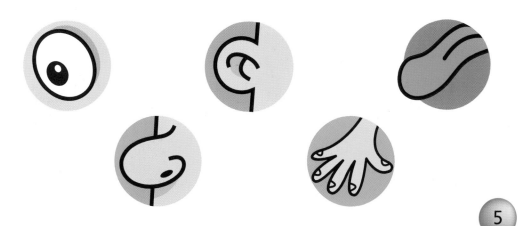

Sorting animals

Class 1 made a list.

✸ Are they all animals?
How do you know?

✸ Cut out the pictures on
Task Sheet 2.

✸ Sort them into groups.

✸ How did you sort them?

✸ Why did you sort them
like this?

✸ Are you an animal? How do
you know?

bird

snail

car

TAXI

fish

elephant

human

worm

cat

hamster

frog

flower

6

ask 5 Growing older

Find a photo of you as a baby and a photo of you now.

YOU NEED:

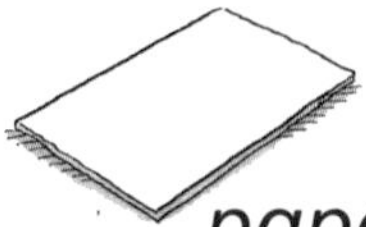

paper

photo of you now

paint

photo of you as a baby

- Now paint a picture of what you think you will look like when you are a grown-up.

- Make a picture gallery of your two photos and painting.

Rhiannon aged 12 weeks

Rhiannon now

- Display all the pictures. Guess who's who.

Animals grow

All animals grow and change.

✿ What will these baby animals grow into?

✿ How will they change?

✿ Think of some animal families.

✿ Make some cards like these.

✿ Play the happy families game.

Amazing frogs

The life cycle of a frog.

These pictures are in the wrong order.

✳ Put the pictures on Task Sheet 3 in the right order.

✳ How will the frogspawn change?

9

Task 8 Size

⚡ Who is the tallest in your class?
How can you find out?

⚡ You could measure your friend's height using art straws. What else could you use?

Class 1 recorded their results in a table like this:

Name	Number of straws high
Ahmed	4 and a bit
Mary	4

⚡ Measure yourself and other children.

⚡ Write your results in a table on Task Sheet 4.

Age and height

✷ Do you think the oldest children in your class are the tallest?

✷ How can you find out?

✷ Which children in your class have the same birthday month as you?

✷ Stand in a line in birthday groups.

✷ Take turns to look at the line.

January

May

✷ Which birthday group is the oldest?

✷ Are the oldest children always the tallest?

Our survey

These children are talking about how they are alike and how they are different.

> My hand is bigger than yours.

> Our eyes are different colours.

> Our hand prints are different.

Share your ideas like this.

✲ How many children in your class have blue eyes? How many brown? How many green?

✲ Use Task Sheet 5 to help you plan a survey.

✲ Now carry out your survey.

Tally chart

★ Record your results in a tally chart like this one. Use Task Sheet 6.

Eye colour	Number of children
blue	✝✝✝ ✝ 5
brown	
green	

★ Use coloured shapes or a computer to make a pictogram.

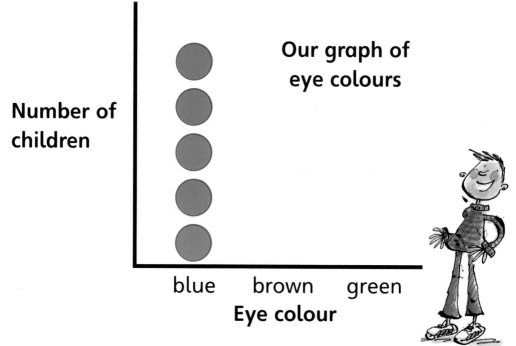

Number of children

Our graph of eye colours

blue   brown   green

Eye colour

★ What does your graph show?

Animals move

Most birds can hop, walk and fly.

✴ Watch a bird.
How does it move?

✴ Draw the bird and write how it moves on Task Sheet 7.

Name of bird	How it moves

✴ How do other animals move?

✴ Which parts of the body do they use to move?

✴ How do you move?

✴ Draw some pictures or make a list.

3 Is it alive?

8

These things have
been collected from
the school grounds.

✳ Which things do you think are alive?

✳ Which things do you think are not alive?

✳ Sort them and draw them in a table.

Alive	Not alive

✳ How can you tell if something is alive?

15

Keeping Clean

Wash my fingers
Wash my toes,
Wash each arm
Wash my nose,
Wash my ankles
Wash each knee,
Wash and dry
All of me.

✣ Make a list of other parts of the body.

✣ Sing the song again with these new words.